Animals of Australia
For Kids
Amazing Animal Books for Young
Readers

By Shawn Vincent Wilson
Mendon Cottage Books

JD-Biz Publishing

Read More Amazing Animal Books

Purchase at Amazon.com

Table of Contents

Introduction 4

What is a Marsupial? 6

Kangaroo 8

Wallaby 10

Tree-Kangaroo 11

Sugar Glider 13

Koala 15

Wombat 17

Other Marsupials 19

Emu 23

Cassowary 27

Egg-laying Mammals 29

    Echidna 29

    Platypus 31

Kookaburra 34

Dingo 36

Publisher 38

Introduction

There are many animals that live all over the world. For instance, rabbits can be found in North America and Europe. Bears live in those places as well as in South America and Asia.

But there are some animals and that live in only one place. In this book we will show you creatures from Australia.

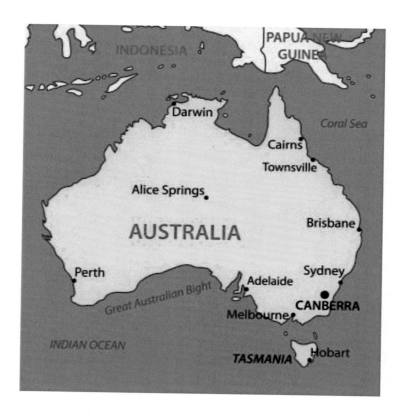

Australia is a continent in the southern part of the world. There are islands nearby, but Australia itself is thousands of miles away from all other continents. That is why many of the animals have never *migrated* (moved) to other continents.

Some of the creatures in this book also live on the islands near Australia, such as New Zealand, New Guinea, and Tasmania.

What is a Marsupial?

A *marsupial* (mar-SOO-pee-al) is a type of animal that has a special way of caring for its young. When a baby marsupial is born, it is too weak and frail to live outside. Instead, it crawls inside a pouch in the mother's body where it can be warm and protected. It stays there until it grows big enough to go outside.

Kangaroos and koalas are marsupials. Most of the Australian animals in this book are marsupials. Marsupials live in other parts of the world too.

A young marsupial is usually called a *joey*. You can sometimes see a joey sticking its head out of its mother's pouch.

All marsupials are *mammals*. This means that the young ones drink milk from their mother's body. Joeys do this while inside their mother's pouch.

Kangaroo

A kangaroo is a large marsupial. (To read more about what that means, click here: _marsupial_.) Kangaroos are famous for the way they move: they hop fast. Mother kangaroos are also famous for the way they carry their babies in a pouch in their bodies. (All marsupials do that, not just kangaroos.)

A kangaroo has big feet, small hands, and a long tail. Kangaroos usually stand bending forward, but they can also stand upright, like humans do. The largest kangaroos can be as tall as a man.

A kangaroo moves by hopping on its powerful legs and long feet. Its long tail helps it balance while it hops. Some kangaroos can move as fast as as 30 mph (48 km/h). This helps them travel long distances to look for food and water.

Kangaroos are *herbivores* (ERB-uh-vors), which mean they eat only plants. They mostly eat grass.

Kangaroos live in groups called *mobs*. Kangaroos in a mob often greet each other by touches their noses together and sniffing.

Male kangaroos in a mob sometimes fight with each other. This fighting is called *boxing* because they hit each other with their hands, but they also wrestle and kick each other too. The males fight over females. They may also fight over a space at a drinking spot. Sometimes they just fight for fun.

Wallaby

A *wallaby* is also a marsupial, but smaller than a <u>kangaroo</u>. Some types are only half as large as a kangaroo. Certain types of wallaby look just like a small kangaroo, but others have faces that look like mice or rats. They all have big feet and long tails.

Tree-Kangaroo

Look at this picture. This animal does not look much like a kangaroo, does it? Its arms and legs are about the same length. And its ears seem too short.

Even so, it is called a *tree-kangaroo*. It is a marsupial, like regular kangaroos, but it is smaller. It does not hop along the ground; it walks slowly and clumsily.

But they do hop – when they are in the trees! They hold the tree trunk with their hands and hop up with their powerful legs. This is how they climb the tree. They can also hop from one tree to the next, even when it is far away. They can even hop down to the ground from a branch six stories high!

Tree-kangaroos live in forests in Australia and on the islands of New Guinea. They eat what they find in the trees: leaves, fruit, even birds eggs.

Sugar Glider

A *sugar glider* is a little possum that can fit in your hands. They can glide through the air like a paper plane!

This possum lives in the trees. When the sugar glider wants to go from one tree to another, it will jump out of the tree and spread all its legs wide. There are flaps of loose skin between its hands and feet. This skin acts like wings, so the possum can glide to the next tree. It steers by bending its arms, legs, and tail.

We call this animal a "sugar" glider because it likes to eat tree sap, nectar, honeydew, and other sweet substances. It also eats insects, grubs, and sometimes small lizards and birds.

Sugar gliders are *nocturnal* (noc-TUR-nal). That means they sleep during the day and are awake at night. Their big eyes help them see in the dark.

Koala

The *koala* (ko-AH-la) is a <u>marsupial</u> that lives in trees. It is about two feet tall, has round fluffy ears, and has no tail, so it looks a little like a teddy bear. That's why people sometimes call it a "koala bear". But it is not really a bear.

Koalas are very picky eaters. They eat leaves from the *eucalyptus* (yu-ca-LIP-tus) tree. They eat almost nothing else, not even other type of leaves. This is interesting, because eucalyptus leaves can be poisonous to other animals. It can even make humans very sick. Yet eucalyptus is safe for koalas.

Koalas are even more picky about drinking than they are about eating. There is moisture in the leaves they eat, so a grown male koala needs to drink only a little water. He finds it in puddles or in the hollows of trees. Female koalas do not drink at all!

Koalas are *nocturnal,* so they sleep all day in a tree. They also sleep most of the night as well. In fact, koalas are only awake for about four hours each night. That's probably less time than you are in school!

Because koalas are marsupials, the joey (baby) lives in its mother's pouch until it is six months old. At that age it is old enough to come out. It likes to ride on its mother's back or cling to her belly until it is a year old.

Wombat

Wombats are chubby, furry <u>marsupials</u>. They have short legs and a short tail. They can be as big as a medium-sized dog. Some wombats grow to be 4 feet long.

Wombats live underground. They dig tunnels using their sharp front claws and front teeth like a rodent's. A wombat tunnel can be up to 100 feet long. The tunnel has more than one exit. It also has side tunnels and special rooms to sleep in. The tunnel is just wide enough for the wombat to fit inside. You might fit in a wombat tunnel yourself.

A wombat may dig several long tunnels to live in. Sometime they will take turns with others. When one wombat leaves a tunnel, another wombat will use it himself.

Wombats also dig short tunnels when they want to rest, or to hide from danger. A wombat can dig so fast, he can get underground even while a bigger animal is trying to catch him.

Wombats are *nocturnal* – they usually stay in their tunnels during the day and come out at night. Sometimes they come out during the day if it is cool or cloudy. They eat grass, and sometimes herbs, bark, or roots. Like koalas, they drink very little water, because there is a lot of moisture in the grass they eat.

You may think that a wombat is lazy. They move around slowly. They sleep a lot. But wombats are not lazy. It is a lot of hard work to dig all those tunnels!

And they can run fast. If a wombat is being chased by a dangerous creature, it can run 25 miles per hour. That's faster than almost any human. It can only run this fast for about 90 seconds, but that is often fast enough to get away from danger. It's so fast, it can knock a grown person down if he's in the way!

Wombats are strong too, and they can jump over things taller than they are. So if a wombat is walking around and comes to a fence, he will not go around it – he'll jump over it, dig under it, or just push through it!

Other Marsupials

There are other <u>marsupials</u> that come from Austraila. These are smaller than kangaroos – and have funny names!

The ***quoll*** (KWALL) can be one or two feet long. It is carnivorous, which means that it eats other animals.

Quolls eat rabbits, small birds, lizards, and insects. They live in rocky dens or hollowed-out logs. Baby quolls are called "puppies", not joeys.

The **_quokka_** (KWAK-ah) is the size of a cat. It can climb small trees and bushes, and eats leaves, stems, and bark.

They are very friendly to people, so they may come close to you instead of run away.

The **rat-kangaroo** is the size of a rabbit. It looks like a big rat or mouse with long feet. It jumps like a <u>kangaroo</u>. It is a marsupial, so it's not really a rat.

(In North America, there really *is* a rat with big feet that jumps. It's called a "kangaroo rat", but it is not the same as a rat-kangaroo!)

The **numbat** is the size of a cat. It has a pointed muzzle and colorful stripes. It eats only termites using its long, sticky tongue. Every day it eats 20,000 termites!

Some people call it a *banded anteater* because of its stripes, but it does not eat ants. Even though the numbat is a marsupial, the mother numbat does not have a pouch. Instead, she has a special spot on her belly surrounded by thick fur. The babies cling to her on this spot.

Emu

The *emu* (EE-moo) is a tall bird that is a like an ostrich, but not as large. A grown emu is almost as tall than a grown human. It is the largest bird in Australia. (Ostriches are from Africa.)

Although the emu is a bird, it cannot fly. But it can run fast. An emu will run up to 30 mph, if it has to get away from eagles, hawks, or other dangerous birds. An emu will also run from *dingos*, which are dangerous wild dogs. But if it cannot get away, it can jump and kick the dingo with its powerful legs and the claws on its feet.

Emus do not always run that fast, but they can run a long way on their long legs. Emus sometimes travel together in a flock when they are all looking for food and water.

They eat many types of plants and insects. But birds have no teeth, so they cannot chew their food. So emus also swallow small and medium-size stones! The stones stay inside their stomach and grind up the food they swallow. Other types of birds also swallow stones for this same reason.

Where emus live, there is not a lot of water to drink. They may go for one or two days without drinking water. When they do find a place with water, they will drink for a long time. They may drink for 10 minutes without stopping!

Many male animals and birds will fight other males in order to impress a female. (That's one reason that kangaroos box, remember?) Emus are different: two females will often fight over a single male.

A mother emu lays her eggs in a nest. The eggs are dark green and 5 inches long. (Have you ever bought a dozen eggs from a store? Those are chicken eggs, of course. That package of eggs weighs as much as one emu's egg!)

Most mother birds sit on the nest to keep the eggs warm. After the chicks hatch, she feeds and takes care of them. But it is different with emus. It is the father emu, not the mother, who sits on the nest, and takes care of the chicks.

Cassowary

The *cassowary* (KASS-uh-ware-ee) is a large bird that cannot fly, like the <u>emu</u>. Some types of cassowary are about 3 feet tall, but the biggest ones are as tall as an emu, and heavier. They live in rainforests in Australia and New Guinea. They are good at hiding from people in the rainforest.

Cassowaries have black feathers. Their heads have no feathers, like head of a turkey. The skin on its head and neck is bright blue.

The pointy organ on top of the cassowary's head is called a *casque* or *helmet*. Females have a larger casque than males. No one is sure what this casque is for. Maybe the casque protects the bird's head when it runs through the dense plants of the rainforest.

Cassowaries eat snails, ferns, seeds, and flowers, but the food they eat the most is fruit. They pick up fruit that has fallen from trees. Maybe the cassowary's casque keeps falling fruit from hitting it on the head.

A cassowary make an unusual noise: it is a loud, low "boom" sound. It is so low, that it is hard for people to hear it. But other cassowaries can hear the boom far away. Maybe the cassowary's casque helps them make this unique noise.

A mother cassowary lays from 3 to 8 eggs in her nest. These eggs are green or bluish green, and each one can be 5 inches long. The male sits on the nest to keep them warm, and the mother goes away to lay more eggs in nest of another male. When the eggs hatch, the males take care of the chicks.

Egg-laying Mammals

Nearly all mammals – such as dogs, cats, kangaroos, cows – give birth to "live young". In other words, they have babies like people do. But there is one kind of mammal that lays eggs, the way that birds and reptiles do.

The word for these creatures is *monotreme* (MON-oh-treem). Monotremes are not marsupials.

There are two types of monotremes: the *echidna* and the *platypus*.

Echidna

The *echidna* is an animal that is covered in spines, like a porcupine. Its mouth is a slender snout or beak. The echidna eats ants and termites, so sometimes it is known as a *spiny anteater.*

One type is called the *short-beaked echidna.* It lives in Australia and grows to be 12-18 inches long. There is also the *long-beaked echidnas* that lives on the island of New Guinea. These can be 2-3 feet long.

The echidna has strong legs and large claws. To catch its food, it tears open soft logs and anthills where termites and ants live. Then it catches the bugs on its sticky tongue.

Its legs and claws make it a strong digger. When it is scared or being chased by a bigger animal, it can quickly dig a long hole, or *burrow,* into the ground to hide in.

Another thing it may do when scared is curl itself into a ball. Its spines will stick out in every direction. Other animals will leave it alone so they don't hurt themselves on the echidna's spines!

Although the echidna is not a marsupial, a mother echidna does have a pouch. She lays her egg directly into the pouch. The egg is soft and rubbery, like a snake's egg, not hard like a bird's egg.

While the egg is in the pouch, the mother echidna digs a burrow to live in.

Ten days after the egg is laid, it hatches inside the pouch. The newborn echidna is called a *puggle,* and it stays inside the pouch for 2-3 months. It's time to leave the pouch when the puggle's spines poke the mother!

The puggle stays in the burrow while its mother leaves to find food. When it is six months old, the young echidna will leave the burrow to live on its own.

Platypus

A platypus is a funny animal. Like a beaver, it is covered in fur, has a broad, flat tail, and spends a lot of its time in the water. Its webbed feet are like those of an otter. But it is also a little like a duck: it has a bill instead of lips and teeth, and lays eggs. Sometimes the platypus is called the *duck-billed platypus.*

When explorers from Europe came to Australia and saw the platypus, they wrote to scientists in Great Britain about the animal. They also sent the body of a platypus to them. The scientists who saw it said "There can't *really* be an animal like this. Someone is playing a trick on us! Maybe they put a duck's bill onto a beaver's body!"

There is one more way that a platypus is not like other mammals: it is poisonous. On the hind feet of the male platypus is a *spur* – a hook made of bone. When it kicks another animal with this spur, it injects its poison into that animal. The poison can kill small animals such as dogs, and can be very painful to humans. If you meet a platypus, you should be very friendly!

The platypus eats insects, shrimp, and crayfish that it catches in the rivers and streams. It closes its eyes, ears, and nose, and dives under the water. The platypus has special organs in its bill that can tell when a little creature is moving, so it doesn't need to see or hear it.

The platypus does not live in the water; it lives in a *burrow,* which is a long hole it digs in the ground. A mother platypus will digs a much longer, deeper burrow, up to 20 yards long, as a place to live and lay her eggs. Platypus eggs are soft and leathery, like a snake or turtle's eggs, not hard like a bird's egg.

When the young platypuses hatch, they are fed by milk from the mother's body. They stay in the burrow while the mother goes out to get food for herself. When the young ones are about four months old, they leave the burrow.

Kookaburra

The *kookaburra* (KOO-ka-BURR-ah) is a bird that lives in Australia, Tasmania, and New Guinea. It is sometimes called the *laughing kookaburra* because it makes a loud noise that sounds like a person laughing.

This bird can grow to be 18 inches long. They make their nests in hollow trees or termite mounds. They live in forests or in trees near towns where people live.

The kookaburra eats mice, snakes, small birds, and small reptiles. Farmers do not like kookaburras because they sometimes catch their chickens or other farm birds. And if someone is having a barbecue, a kookaburra may even steal meat right off of the grill – even if it's hot! But the kookaburra doesn't need to drink water: it gets all the moisture it needs from the food it eats.

Kookaburras live in family groups. When newborn chicks are hatched, their older brothers and sisters help feed and take care of them.

Dingo

The *dingo* is a wild dog that lives on the grasslands, in deserts, and near the edge of forests. Most dingoes are golden or reddish colored, and their eyes are bright yellow or orange.

A dingo lives in a *den*, which is usually a hole he or she digs into the ground. Sometimes a den will be in a hollow log, or underneath some boulders. Sometimes a dingo will move into a burrow where rabbits or wombats used to live.

A dingo will travel long distances from its den in order to find food. A dingo will wade in water, but will not swim. Dingoes can do one thing that most dogs can't do: they can climb trees!

Some dingoes live alone, but others live together in a *pack*. There may be up to 12 dingoes in a pack. The male and female leaders of the pack are called the *alpha pair*. Only the alpha pair has pups. The other adults in the pack help take care of these pups.

Dingoes are *carnivorous,* which means they hunt and kill other animals for food. A dingo that lives alone catches small animals such as rabbits, wallabies, rodents, and even pet cats. Dingoes in a pack work together to catch larger animals, such as kangaroos, wallabies, and cattle.

Dingoes probably prefer to eat meat, but they will also eat fruit and plants. Those that live near people will take food from garbage cans, picnic areas, campsites, and other places we leave leftovers.

Publisher

JD-Biz Corp

P O Box 374

Mendon, Utah 84325

http://www.jd-biz.com/

Mendon Cottage Books

P O Box 374, Mendon Utah 84325

Animals of Australia for Kids

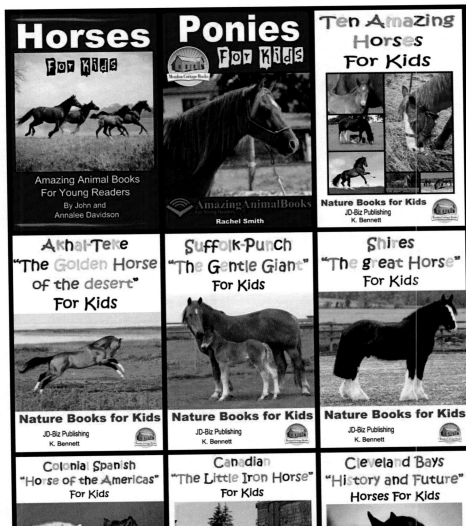

Horses
For Kids

Amazing Animal Books
For Young Readers
By John and
Annalee Davidson

Ponies
For Kids

Meadow Cottage Books

Amazing Animal Books
For Young Readers

Rachel Smith

Ten Amazing
Horses
For Kids

Nature Books for Kids
JD-Biz Publishing
K. Bennett

Akhal-Teke
"The Golden Horse
of the desert"
For Kids

Nature Books for Kids
JD-Biz Publishing
K. Bennett

Suffolk-Punch
"The Gentle Giant"
For Kids

Nature Books for Kids
JD-Biz Publishing
K. Bennett

Shires
"The great Horse"
For Kids

Nature Books for Kids
JD-Biz Publishing
K. Bennett

Colonial Spanish
"Horse of the Americas"
For Kids

Nature Books for Kids
JD-Biz Publishing
K. Bennett

Canadian
"The Little Iron Horse"
For Kids

Nature Books for Kids
JD-Biz Publishing
K. Bennett

Cleveland Bays
"History and Future"
Horses For Kids

Nature Books for Kids
JD-Biz Publishing
K. Bennett

Top Ten Dog Breeds
For Kids
Amazing Animal Books
For Young Readers
Kisha Bennett & John Davidson

German Shepherds
Dog Books for Kids
K. Bennett

Bulldogs
Dog Books for Kids
K. Bennett

Dachshund
Dog Books for Kids
K. Bennett

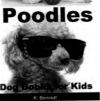
Poodles
Dog Books for Kids
K. Bennett

Labrador Retrievers
Dog Books for Kids
K. Bennett

Rottweilers
Dog Books for Kids
K. Bennett

Boxers
Dog Books for Kids
K. Bennett

Golden Retrievers
Dog Books for Kids
K. Bennett

Puppies
Dog Books For Kids
Amazing Animal Books
By John Davidson

Beagles
Dog Books for Kids
K. Bennett

Yorkshire Terriers
Dog Books for Kids
K. Bennett

Dogs
Top Ten Dog Breeds
For Kids
Amazing Animal Books
For Young Readers
Zahra Jazeel & John Davidson

Cats
For Kids
Amazing Animal Books
For Young Readers
K. Bennett & John Davidson

Foxes
For Kids
Amazing Animal Books
For Young Readers
Zahra Jazeel & John Davidson

Wolves
For Kids
Amazing Animal Books
For Young Readers
By John Davidson and Virginia Fidler

Monkeys

Amazing Animal Books
For Young Readers
By John and
Annalee Davidson

Whales

Amazing Animal Books
For Young Readers
By John Davidson

Kittens

Amazing Animal Books
For Young Readers
By John Davidson

Meerkats
For Kids
Amazing Animal Books
For Young Readers
John Davidson and Lisa Barry

Elephants
For Kids

Amazing Animal Books
For Young Readers
Kim Chase & John Davidson

**Big Mammals
of Yellowstone**
For Kids

Amazing Animal Books
For Young Readers
By John Davidson

Big Cats
For Kids
Amazing Animal Books
For Young Readers
By John Davidson

My First Book About
Pandas

Amazing Animal Books BEST
By Annalee and John Davidson
Children's Picture Books

Chinchillas

For Kids
Amazing Animal Books
For Young Readers
John Davidson and Jaimie Rhynsburger

Beavers
For Kids

Amazing Animal Books
For Young Readers
By J Davidson

Bees

Amazing Animal Books
For Young Readers
By J Davidson and Jennifer Lapointe

**Animals of
Australia**
For Kids
AUSTRALIA
Amazing Animal Books
For Young Readers
By John Davidson
and Shawn Vincent Wilson

Frogs
For Kids
Amazing Animal Books
For Young Readers
By John Davidson

My First Book About
Frogs
Amazing Animal Books
By John Davidson
Children's Picture Books

Tigers
For Kids

Amazing Animal Books
For Young Readers
Kim Chase & John Davidson

Scorpions
For Kids

Amazing Animal Books
For Young Readers
John Davidson

Snakes

For Kids
Amazing Animal Books
For Young Readers
By John Davidson and Nadine Trexla

Animals of Africa
For Kids

Amazing Animal Books
For Young Readers
Steve Muturi & John Davidson

Dinosaurs

For Kids
Amazing Animal Books
For Young Readers
By John Davidson

Sharks

For Kids
Amazing Animal Books
For Young Readers
By John Davidson

Spiders
For Kids

Amazing Animal Books
For Young Readers
By John Davidson

**Giant Panda
Bears**

Amazing Animal Books
For Young Readers
By John Davidson

Giraffes
For Kids

Amazing Animal Books
For Young Readers
Valeria Arcas & John Davidson

Eagles

For Kids
Amazing Animal Books
For Young Readers
Nicholas Williams & John Davidson

Bears
For Kids

Amazing Animal Books
For Young Readers
Zahra Jazeel & John Davidson

Horses
For Kids

Amazing Animal Books
For Young Readers
By John and
Annalee Davidson

Wolves
For Kids

Amazing Animal Books
For Young Readers
By John Davidson and Virginia Fidler

Lady Bugs
For Kids

Amazing Animal Books
For Young Readers
By Jean Hall & John Davidson

Sasquatch - Yeti
Abominable Snowman
Bigfoot
For Kids

Amazing Animal Books
For Young Readers
By John Davidson

Penguins
For Kids

Amazing Animal Books
For Young Readers
Kim Chase & John Davidson

Komodo
Dragons
For Kids

Amazing Animal Books
For Young Readers
By Lisa Barry & John Davidson

Cats
For Kids

Amazing Animal Books
For Young Readers
K. Bennett & John Davidson

Spiders

Amazing Animal Books
For Young Readers
By John Davidson

Giant Panda
Bears

Amazing Animal Books
For Young Readers
By John Davidson

Animals of
North America

Amazing Animal Books
For Young Readers
By John Davidson

Birds of
North America
For Kids

Amazing Animal Books
For Young Readers
By John Davidson

Dolphins
For Kids

Amazing Animal Books
For Young Readers
By John Davidson and Natalia Asfar

Hamsters

For Kids

Amazing Animal Books
For Young Readers
John Davidson

Polar Bears

For Kids

Amazing Animal Books
For Young Readers
By John Davidson and Kim Chase

Turtles
For Kids

Amazing Animal Books
For Young Readers
By John Davidson and Natalia Asfar

Walruses
For Kids

Amazing Animal Books
For Young Readers
By John Davidson and Kim Chase

My First Book About
Animals of
Australia

Amazing Animal Books
By Annalee and John Davidson
Children's Picture Books

Goats
For Kids

Amazing Animal Books
For Young Readers
Rachel Smith & John Davidson

Flamingos
For Kids

Amazing Animal Books
For Young Readers
K. Bennett & John Davidson

Giraffes
For Kids

Amazing Animal Books
For Young Readers
Valeria Arcas & John Davidson

Eagles

For Kids

Amazing Animal Books
For Young Readers
Nicholas Williams & John Davidson

Bears
For Kids

Amazing Animal Books
For Young Readers
Zahra Jazsel & John Davidson

Parrots
For Kids

Amazing Animal Books
For Young Readers
Zahra Jazsel & John Davidson

My First Book About
Kittens

Amazing Animal Books
By John Davidson
Children's Picture Books

Sharks

For Kids

Amazing Animal Books
For Young Readers
By John Davidson

25640490R00027

Made in the USA
Middletown, DE
05 November 2015